Table of Contents

Introduction

Instant Pot has released an 11-in-1 multipurpose cooking appliance that is nothing short of a technological marvel among household appliances. The Instant Pot Duo Crisp Air Fryer combines all of the essential cooking features in one pot. You can now bake, air fry, pressure cook, slow cook, sous vide, sauté, dehydrate, broil, or roast your food all in one pot. In addition, instant Pot has brought incredible technology to your fingertips with the changeable lid function. The details shared in this cookbook acknowledge Instant Pot's mastery and will let you understand how to put both of its lids to good use. You can also learn how to get the most out of this super-efficient cooking appliance with the help of a collection of my recipes.

MEET THE INSTANT POT DUO CRISP AIR FRYER

The Instant Pot Duo Crisp Air Fryer combines the functions of a pressure cooker and an air fryer; it contains a basic display panel, an auto-sealing pressure cooker top, and a separate lid that can be used as an air fryer. The Instant Pot Duo Crisp Air Fryer, a hybrid electric pressure cooker and air fryer, was released in late 2019 and combined two of the most popular kitchen appliances of the last decade into one huge gadget. Those who are not great fans of air fryers but love the Instant Pot, for them, the two were combined, to see rather combining the two was worth it. It is a machine with an 8-quat size with two different lids; one is for air frying, and the other is for pressure cooking. The instant duo performs both functions conveniently.

BENEFITS OF USING INSTANT POT DUO CRISP AIR FRYER:

Instant Pot duo air fryer is a multi-tasker product as it works as a pressure cooker and an air fryer, and it is very convenient for preparing a one-pot meal. Other benefits of this appliance include:

- It has 11-IN-one functionality from air fry, roast, bake, dehydrate, pressure cook, slow cook, rice cooker, yogurt maker, steamer, sauté pan, yogurt maker, sterilizer to food warmer.
- The Duo Crisp can pressure cook an entire chicken till it is tender, and after, it can brown its skin or quickly reheat a small bunch of frozen fries.
- It is reasonably designed; when you need to toss the food inside, you may effortlessly grab the removable air-fryer basket using oven mittens.
- Although the air fryer lid is weighty, it is completely detachable, making it much easier to use, clean, and carry in the kitchen.
- It is also quieter than other air fryers while cooking.
- The multi-level frying basket of the Duo Crisp provides extra surface area for cooking frozen French fries, tots, and nuggets.
- The duo will alert you that it's time to rotate the meal when you're halfway through. This equipment air fries food just as well as a conventional air fryer appliance.
- When you don't have the space or time to set up the oven, the baking option on the Instant Pot Duo Crisp Air Fryer is ideal for cooking.
- It has a versatile inner cooking pot with an anti-spin construction that secures the pot for ideal sautéing and a food-grade stainless-steel cooking pot with a triply bottom for more even cooking.

It can cook for 8 people for large families and in batches for small ones. Instant Pot also has over 10 safety features, additionally overheat protection and a safe locking lid.

STRUCTURAL DESIGN OF INSTANT POT DUO AIR FRYER:

As discussed earlier, the Instant Pot Duo Crisp Air Fryer comes with two lids former lid is for the pressure cooker, and the latter is used for the air fryer. It is composed of four parts:

- **Base unit**: The heating element, control panel, and associated power line are all housed within the stainless steel exterior; it is also called the outer pot.
- **Inner Pot**: Stainless steel pot that can be removed. The inner pot is friendly with the stove as a regular pot on your stovetop. This can be cleaned by both hands or in the dishwasher.
- **Pressure Cooker Lid:** It shuts and seals the Instant Pot under pressure. This lid can be hand-washed or rinsed in the dishwasher.
- **Air fryer lid:** Converts the Instant Pot into an air fryer by closing it. It is not recommended that the lid be washed. Once cool, clean the heating element cover and surrounding area with a gentle, wet cloth or sponge to remove all food particles and grease splatter.

Three Timers:

There are three different timers in Instant Pot:

Cooking Timer: it is for counting cooking time; the display goes on after the Instant pot is pressurized to set cooking time, and then the timer goes down from programmed cooking time. After that, keep warm mode in on.

Keep Warmer Timer: it tells the time for which the food is kept warm in Instant Pot. This timer only activates when the keep warm function is turned on, and the timer counts up from 00.00 till you press the Cancel button. It keeps food warm even though you are not pressure cooking.

Delay Start Timer: this timer allows you to set a time for cooking in the future. It starts counting down once the timer is set. First, select the cooking program, pressure level, and Delay start timer (enter the time when you won't start cooking); press the Start button after that.

HOW DOES PRESSURE COOKER LID WORK?

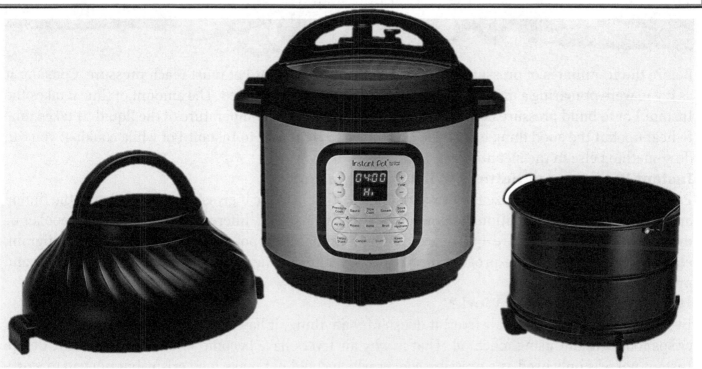

The pressure cooker Instant Pot Duo Crisp Air Fryer produces a controlled atmosphere in which steam builds up in a tightly closed pot. This causes the internal temperature to increase and the pressure to rise as a result. The fiber in the food is tenderized under high pressure, and tastes develop quickly. Because of the pace of cooking, nutrient-rich steam condenses in the pot rather than evaporating, retaining nutritional content. It consists of:

1. As it goes by its name, the sealing ring helps build pressure in Instant Pot by sealing the food tightly, which is heated at a high temperature. This ring can be washed by hands or dishwasher.
2. A trivet or steam rack is used to keep food above the liquid and when you are cooking pot in pot. This can be washed by hands or dishwasher.
3. Condensation Collector collects drops from the lid's condensation; mounts to the back of the base unit. It can be hand-washed or washed in the dishwasher's top rack.

How to release pressure on the Instant Pot?

Pressure on the Instant pot can be released in different ways:

It can be done through Natural Release (NR), in which you allow pressure cooking to complete, float valve to drop, and when pressure comes down, press the Cancel button. It takes 5 to 30 minutes to release natural pressure.

It can be released by Quick Release (QR); after pressure cooking is done, put on a steam venting mechanism to release the pressure manually, and then press the Cancel button. Keep face and hands away from steam

How much time is required to pre-heat Instant Pot?

Before the 10 minutes of pressure cooking can begin, the Instant Pot must reach pressure. Consider it as if you were preparing a meal in an oven that needed to be preheated. The amount of time it takes the Instant Pot to build pressure is determined by the quantity and temperature of the liquid. It takes time to heat up, but the good thing is that you don't have to right next to Instant Pot while cooking; you can do something else in the meantime.

Instant Pot has many buttons. What do they mean?

People usually prefer to utilize the Pressure Cook setting because it gives more control over the timing and pressure levels. In addition, it allows individuals who own a different brand of pressure cooker or multi-cooker to adapt to its recipes quickly. Other buttons on the pot, like Rice, Meat, Meat, Multigrain, etc., are just preset and pre-programmed buttons, like microwaves have, it defines cooking time and pressure levels.

How Does Air Fryer Lid Work?

Even though it's termed an air fryer, it doesn't fry anything; it has the exact opposite effect; rather, it crisps food without using much oil. That is why air fryers have become so common recently. Before Instant pot was only used as a pressure cooker which could not make food crispy but now no to worry as an air fryer lid is introduced in the instant pot, it has turntables as it can be used as a pressure cooker and air fryer lid that crisp or brown the food as per your wish. First, food is put into a mesh basket that is placed in the inner pot. Then the air fryer lid is put on top of it after being heated at a high temperature to make food crispy. It also cooks food, whether it is fresh or frozen. It consists of:

1. For using Instant Pot as an air fryer, it has an Air Fryer Lid.
2. A protective cooling pad is required to protect the surface from the air fryer lid's hot heating element. Place the air fryer cover on this base at all times.
3. Dehydrating or Broil Tray, when air frying two levels of food, this is the tool you utilize. The broil tray is put halfway up in the "Air Fryer Basket" and sits on a ridge.
4. An "Air Fryer Basket" is required at the bottom of the basket, features vents and a ridge where the dehydrating/broil tray can be inserted.
5. "Air Fryer Basket" Base is a base that is raised and clipped onto the "Air Fryer Basket."

FREQUENTLY ASKED QUESTIONS

Here are some tips and frequently asked questions that will help you answer your queries for beginners who will start using Duo Crisp Air fryer.

1. Is it safe for use?

If you have never used a pressure cooker or had a bad experience, it is natural to feel uneasy about starting using it. But for consumer safety, Instant pot loads with safety features like automatic temperature and pressure controls. In addition, the lid is locked, shut-off fuses, and overheat protection, so no need to worry; it is safe for use.

2. What is Instant Pot manual mode?

When you go through recipes of Instant Pot, it mentions a manual button; on the older model, there is a button of Manual button, but on the newer model, the word manual is replaced with Pressure cook in settings. So, don't get confused when your recipe mentions Manual mode; simply use Pressure cook.

3. When pressure comes, the Instant Pot Hiss and Leak. Is it okay?

Yes, it is normal to hiss or leak when pressure is built, but you should notice little to no steam coming out of either the float valve or the steam release mechanism once the float valve has popped up. The sealing ring has most likely been set incorrectly if steam is seeping from the sides of the lid (where the sealing ring sits). Or, if it continues hissing, you should read the troubleshooting section in the manual.

4. If Instant Pot shows 'ON,' what to do?

The Instant Pot's screen will read 'On' after you've programmed it to start pressure cooking. It will stay on until the Instant Pot has reached pressure. It may take a few minutes for the Instant Pot display to shift from 'On' to counting down the pressure cooking time when the float valve is raised.

5. Why Instant Pot makes a clicking noise while cooking?

There seem to be two possible explanations for why the Instant Pot makes clicking noises while functioning. One explanation is that the outside of the inner pot is moist. Before putting an inner pot in the Instant Pot device, make sure it is completely dry. The second explanation for the clicking sounds is that the Instant Pot uses power switching to regulate power inside. It is quite normal, and you should not be concerned.

6. Minimum quantity of liquid required in Instant Pot and for double recipes is it necessary to double cooking time?

To come to pressure, the Instant Pot needs steam and liquid. The Instant Pot company has stated that 1/2 to 2 cups is recommended. As time passes and through an experience, you will determine how much liquid is required for different recipes.

Secondly, you don't have to change the cooking time when you double a recipe. This is because the density and thickness of the ingredients, rather than their weight, determine the cooking time.

CHAPTER 1

BREAKFAST

EGGS IN AVOCADO CUPS

Preparation Time: 10 mins   **Cooking Time:** 10 mins   **Servings:** 2

Ingredients:

- Non-stick cooking spray
- 1 avocado, halved and pitted
- Salt and ground black pepper, as required
- 2 eggs
- 1 tablespoon Parmesan cheese, shredded

Directions:

1. Grease a square piece of foil with cooking spray and then arrange in "Air Fryer Basket."
2. Arrange the "Air Fryer Basket" in the pot of Instant Pot Duo Crisp Air Fryer.
3. Cover the pot with "Air Fryer Lid" and seal it.
4. Select "Bake" and set the temperature to 390 °F for 12 minutes.
5. Press "Start" to begin preheating.
6. Meanwhile, scoop out about 2 teaspoons of flesh from each avocado half.
7. Crack 1 egg in each avocado half and sprinkle with salt and black pepper.
8. When the unit shows "Hot" instead of "On," open the lid and place the avocado halves into the basket.
9. Again, cover the pot with "Air Fryer Lid" and seal it.
10. Press "Start" to begin cooking.
11. Open the lid and transfer the avocado halves onto serving plates when cooking time is completed.
12. Top with Parmesan and serve.

Nutritional Information per Serving:

Calories: 278, Fat: 24.7g, Net Carbohydrates: 2.4g, Carbohydrates: 9.1g, Fiber: 6.7g, Sugar: 0.8g, Protein: 8.4g, Sodium: 188mg

SAUSAGE & BACON OMELET

Preparation Time: 10 minutes   Cooking Time: 10 minutes   Servings: 2

Ingredients:

- 4 eggs
- 1 bacon slice, chopped
- 2 sausages, chopped
- 1 yellow onion, chopped

Directions:

1. Arrange the "Air Fryer Basket" in the pot of Instant Pot Duo Crisp Air Fryer.
2. Cover the pot with "Air Fryer Lid" and seal it.
3. Select "Air Fry" and set the temperature to 320 °F for 10 minutes.
4. Press "Start" to begin preheating.
5. In a bowl, crack the eggs and beat them well.
6. Add the remaining ingredients and gently stir to combine.
7. Place the mixture into a baking pan.
8. When the unit shows "Hot" instead of "On," open the lid and place the pan into the "Air Fryer Basket."
9. Again, cover the pot with "Air Fryer Lid" and seal it.
10. Press "Start" to begin cooking.
11. Open the lid and transfer the omelet onto a plate when cooking time is completed.
12. Cut into equal-sized wedges and serve hot.

Nutritional Information per Serving:

Calories: 508, Fat: 38.4g, Net Carbohydrates: 4.8g, Carbohydrates: 6g, Fiber: 1.2g, Sugar: 3g, Protein: 33.2g, Sodium: 1082mg

OAT & SEED GRANOLA

Preparation Time: 15 minutes   Cooking Time: 2½ hours   Servings: 6

Ingredients:

- Non-stick cooking spray
- ½ cup sunflower kernels
- 5 cups rolled oats
- 2 tablespoons ground flax seeds
- ¾ cup applesauce

- ¼ cup olive oil
- ¼ cup unsalted butter
- 1 teaspoon ground cinnamon
- ½ cup dates, pitted and chopped finely
- ½ cup golden raisins

Directions:

1. Grease the pot of Instant Pot Duo Crisp Air Fryer with the cooking spray generously.
2. Add sunflower kernels, rolled oats, flax seeds, applesauce, oil, butter and cinnamon in the prepared pot and stir to combine.
3. Cover the pot with "Air Fryer Lid" and seal it.
4. Select "Slow Cook" and set the time for 2½ hours.
5. Press "Start" to begin cooking.
6. Open the lid and transfer the granola onto a large baking sheet when cooking time is completed.
7. Add the dates and raisins and stir to combine.
8. Set aside to cool completely before serving.
9. You can preserve this granola in an airtight container.

Nutritional Information per Serving:

Calories: 189, Fat: 10g, Net Carbohydrates: 23.7g, Carbohydrates: 27.7g, Fiber: 4g, Sugar: 7.7g, Protein: 4.6g, Sodium: 3mg

QUINOA PORRIDGE

Preparation Time: 10 minutes   Cooking Time: 1 minute   Servings: 6

Ingredients:

- 11¼ cups water
- 1 cup fresh apple juice
- 1½ cups uncooked quinoa, rinsed
- 1 tablespoon honey
- 1 cinnamon stick
- Pinch of salt

Directions:

1. In the pot of Instant Pot Duo Crisp Air Fryer, add all ingredients and stir to combine well.
2. Cover the pot with "Pressure Lid" and seal it.
3. Select "Pressure" and set the time for 1 minute.
4. Press "Start" to begin cooking.
5. When cooking time is completed, do a "Quick" release.
6. Open the lid, and with a fork, fluff the quinoa.
7. Serve warm.

Nutritional Information per Serving:

Calories: 186, Fat: 2.5g, Net Carbohydrates: 31.7g, Carbohydrates: 34.8g, Fiber: 3.1g, Sugar: 6.9g, Protein: 6g, Sodium: 31mg

BLUEBERRY MUFFINS

Preparation Time: 15 minutes   Cooking Time: 25 minutes   Servings: 6

Ingredients:

- Non-stick cooking spray
- 1/3 cup whole-wheat flour
- 1/3 cup cornmeal
- 2 teaspoons baking powder
- ½ teaspoon ground cinnamon
- ¼ teaspoon salt
- 1 large egg
- ½ cup buttermilk
- 2 tablespoons unsweetened applesauce
- 2 tablespoons sugar
- ½ cup fresh blueberries

Directions:

1. Grease 6 cups of a muffin tin with cooking spray and set aside.
2. Mix the flour, cornmeal, baking powder, cinnamon, and salt in a bowl.
3. Place the egg, buttermilk, applesauce, and sugar in a small bowl and beat until well combined.
4. Add the flour mixture and mix until just combined.
5. Gently, fold in the blueberries.
6. Divide the mixture into prepared muffin cups evenly.
7. Arrange the "Multi-Functional Rack" in the pot of Instant Pot Duo Crisp Air Fryer.
8. Cover the pot with "Air Fryer Lid" and seal it.
9. Select "Bake" and set the temperature to 350 °F for 25 minutes.
10. Press "Start" to begin preheating.
11. When the unit shows "Hot" instead of "On," open the lid and place the muffin tin over the rack.
12. Again, cover the pot with "Air Fryer Lid" and seal it.
13. Press "Start" to begin cooking.
14. When cooking time is completed, open the lid and place the muffin tin onto a wire rack to cool for about 10 minutes.
15. Carefully invert the muffins onto the wire rack to completely cool before serving.

Nutritional Information per Serving:

Calories: 96, Fat: 1.4g, Net Carbohydrates: 17.7g, Carbohydrates: 18.8g, Fiber: 1.2g, Sugar: 6.8g, Protein: 3.1g, Sodium: 134mg

CHAPTER 2

GRAINS & BEANS

QUINOA WITH TOFU

 Preparation Time: 15 minutes

 Cooking Time: 7 minutes

 Servings: 8

Ingredients:

- 1 tablespoon olive oil
- 1 large onion, chopped
- 1 cup uncooked quinoa, rinsed
- 2 garlic cloves, minced
- ½ teaspoon fresh ginger, grated
- 1 teaspoon ground turmeric
- 1 teaspoon ground cumin
- 1 teaspoon ground coriander
- 2 cups vegetable broth
- 12-ounce firm tofu, pressed, drained and cut into ½-inch cubes
- 2 bell peppers, seeded and chopped
- 4 cups cauliflower rice
- ¼ cup fresh cilantro leaves
- ¼ cup almonds, toasted sliced
- 3 tablespoons fresh lemon juice
- Salt and ground black pepper, as required

Directions:

1. In the pot of Instant Pot Duo Crisp, place the oil and press "Sauté."
2. Press "Start" to begin cooking and heat for about 2-3 minutes.
3. Now add the onion and cook for about 2-3 minutes.
4. Add the quinoa, garlic and ginger and cook for about 1-2 minutes.
5. Stir in the spices, salt and pepper and cook for about 30 seconds.
6. Stir in 2 tablespoons of broth and scrape the brown bits from the bottom.
7. Press "Cancel" to stop cooking and stir in the tofu, bell pepper and remaining broth.
8. Cover the pot with "Pressure Lid" and seal it.
9. Select "Pressure" and set the time for 1 minute.
10. Press "Start" to begin cooking.
11. When cooking time is completed, do a "Natural" release.
12. Open the lid and stir in the cauliflower rice.
13. Immediately cover the pot with "Pressure Lid" for about 5 minutes.
14. Open the lid and stir in the almond, cilantro, lemon juice.
15. Serve warm

Nutritional Information per Serving:

Calories: 178, Fat: 6.6g, Net Carbohydrates: 18.3g, Carbohydrates: 22.7g, Fiber: 4.4g, Sugar: 4g, Protein: 9.3g, Sodium: 62mg

LENTILS WITH SPINACH

Preparation Time: 15 minutes   Cooking Time: 19 minutes   Servings: 6

Ingredients:

- 1 tablespoon olive oil
- 1 onion, chopped
- 4 garlic cloves, minced
- 1 teaspoon fresh ginger, minced
- 1 (14½-ounce) can crushed tomatoes
- 1 (13½-ounce) can light coconut milk
- 2 cups dry red lentils, rinsed
- 3 tablespoons tomato paste
- 2½ tablespoons curry powder
- 1 teaspoon smoked paprika
- ½ teaspoon cayenne pepper
- 1 cup fresh spinach, chopped

Directions:

1. In the pot of Instant Pot Duo Crisp Air Fryer, place the oil and press "Sauté."
2. Press "Start" to begin cooking and heat for about 2-3 minutes.
3. Now add the onion, garlic and ginger and cook for about 2-4 minutes.
4. Press "Cancel" to stop cooking and stir in the remaining ingredients except for spinach.
5. Cover the pot with "Pressure Lid" and seal it.
6. Select "Pressure" and set the time for 15 minutes.
7. Press "Start" to begin cooking.
8. When cooking time is completed, do a "Natural" release.
9. Open the lid and stir in the spinach.
10. Immediately cover the pot with "Pressure Lid" for about 5 minutes.
11. Open the lid and serve immediately.

Nutritional Information per Serving:

Calories: 181, Fat: 3.6g, Net Carbohydrates: 19.2g, Carbohydrates: 28.6g, Fiber: 9.4g, Sugar: 6.3g, Protein: 10.5g, Sodium: 696mg

CHICKPEAS CURRY

Preparation Time: 10 minutes

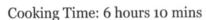

Cooking Time: 6 hours 10 mins

Servings: 6

Ingredients:

- 1 tablespoon butter
- 2 medium onions, chopped
- 1 tablespoon fresh ginger, minced
- 2 garlic cloves, minced
- 2 jalapeño peppers, seeded and chopped finely
- 2 teaspoons ground cumin
- 1 teaspoon ground coriander
- 2 teaspoons paprika
- 1 teaspoon ground turmeric

- 1 teaspoon ground cinnamon
- 1 (14-ounce) can diced tomatoes with juice
- 30 ounces canned chickpeas, drained and rinsed
- 2/3 cup vegetable broth
- Salt and ground black pepper, as required
- 2 tablespoons fresh lemon juice
- 4 tablespoons fresh cilantro, chopped

Directions:

1. In the pot of Instant Pot Duo Crisp Air Fryer, place the butter and press "Sauté."
2. Press "Start" to begin cooking and heat for about 2-3 minutes.
3. Now add the onion and cook for about 8-9 minutes.
4. Add the ginger, garlic, jalapeño peppers and spices and cook for about 1 minute.
5. Add the tomatoes with juice and stir to combine.
6. Press "Cancel" to stop cooking and stir in the remaining ingredients except for lemon juice and cilantro.
7. Cover the pot with "Air Fryer Lid" and seal it.
8. Select "Slow Cook" and set the time for 6 hours.
9. Press "Start" to begin cooking.
10. Open the lid and stir in the lemon juice when cooking time is completed.
11. Serve hot with the garnishing of cilantro.

Nutritional Information per Serving:

Calories: 231, Fat: 4.3g, Net Carbohydrates: 32g, Carbohydrates: 40.8g, Fiber: 8.8g, Sugar: 3.8g, Protein: 9.1g, Sodium: 653mg

BEANS & QUINOA CHILI

Preparation Time: 15 minutes   Cooking Time: 6 hours 10 mins   Servings: 6

Ingredients:

- 2 teaspoons olive oil
- 1 large yellow onion, chopped
- 2 celery stalks, chopped
- 3 garlic cloves, chopped
- ¼ cup water
- 2 tablespoons tomato paste
- 1½ tablespoons chipotle in adobo, chopped finely
- 2 teaspoons chili powder
- 1 teaspoon ground coriander
- 1 teaspoon ground cumin
- ½ teaspoon ground cinnamon
- ½ teaspoon smoked paprika
- Pinch of cayenne pepper
- 3 cups vegetable broth
- 3 cups cooked black beans
- 1 cup uncooked quinoa, rinsed
- 1-1¼ pound butternut squash, peeled and cubed
- 1 (15-ounce) can fire-roasted, diced tomatoes with juice
- 1 small avocado, peeled, pitted and sliced

Directions:

1. In the pot of Instant Pot Duo Crisp Air Fryer, place the oil and press "Sauté."
2. Press "Start" to begin cooking and heat for about 2-3 minutes.
3. Add the onion and celery and cook for about 5-6 minutes.
4. Add the garlic and cook for about 1 minute.
5. Add the water, tomato paste, chipotle and spices and cook for about 1 minute, stirring continuously.
6. Press "Cancel" to stop cooking and stir in the broth, black beans, quinoa, squash and tomatoes with juice.
7. Cover the pot with "Air Fryer Lid" and seal it.
8. Select "Slow Cook" and set the time for 6 hours.
9. Press "Start" to begin cooking.
10. When cooking time is completed, open the lid and serve hot with the topping of avocado slices.

Nutritional Information per Serving:

Calories: 397, Fat: 11.5g, Net Carbohydrates: 44.8g, Carbohydrates: 60.6g, Fiber: 15.8g ,Sugar: 6.4g, Protein: 17.1g, Sodium: 414mg

BEANS & VEGGIE BURGERS

Preparation Time: 15 minutes

Cooking Time: 21 minutes

Servings: 4

Ingredients:
- 1 cup cooked black bean
- 2 cups boiled potatoes, peeled and mashed
- 1 cup fresh spinach, chopped
- 1 cup fresh mushrooms, chopped
- 2 teaspoons Chili lime seasoning
- Non-stick cooking spray

Directions:
1. In a large bowl, add the beans, potatoes, spinach, mushrooms, seasoning, and mix until well combined with your hands.
2. Make 4 equal-sized patties from the mixture.
3. Grease the "Air Fryer Basket" with cooking spray and then arrange in the pot of Instant Pot Duo Crisp Air Fryer.
4. Cover the pot with "Air Fryer Lid" and seal it.
5. Select "Air Fry" and set the temperature to 370 °F for 18 minutes.
6. Press "Start" to begin preheating.
7. When the unit shows "Hot" instead of "On," open the lid and place the patties into "Air Fryer Basket."
8. Spray each patty with the cooking spray
9. Again, cover the pot with "Air Fryer Lid" and seal it.
10. Press "Start" to begin cooking.
11. While cooking, flip the patties once after 12 minutes.
12. After 18 minutes of cooking, set the temperature to 390 °F for 3 minutes.
13. When cooking time is completed, open the lid and serve hot.

Nutritional Information per Serving:
Calories: 114, Fat: 0.4g, Net Carbohydrates: 16.9g, Carbohydrates: 22.8g, Fiber: 5.9g, Sugar: 1.2g, Protein: 5.8g, Sodium: 120mg

CHAPTER 3
SIDE DISHES

GARLICKY BRUSSELS SPROUT

Preparation Time: 10 minutes

Cooking Time: 1 hour 6 mins

Servings: 4

Ingredients:

- 1 tablespoon olive oil
- 2 garlic cloves, minced
- Salt and ground black pepper, as required
- 1 pound Brussels sprouts, cut in half

Directions:

1. Fill the Instant Pot Duo Crisp Air Fryer pot with water up to ½-full of the mark.
2. Select "Sous Vide" and set the temperature to 180 °F for 1 hour.
3. Cover the pot with "Pressure Lid" and seal it.
4. Press "Start" to begin preheating.
5. Meanwhile, add all ingredients except Brussel sprouts in a bowl and mix until well combined.
6. In a cooking pouch, place Brussels sprouts and oil mixture.
7. Seal the pouch tightly after squeezing out the excess air.
8. When the unit shows "Hot" instead of "On," open the lid and place the pouch in the pot.
9. Again, cover the pot with "Pressure Lid" and seal it.
10. Press "Start" to begin cooking.
11. Open the lid and remove the pouch from the inner pot when the cooking time is completed.
12. Carefully open the pouch and serve immediately.

Nutritional Information per Serving:

Calories: 81, Fat: 3.9g, Net Carbohydrates: 6.5g, Carbohydrates: 10.8g, Fiber: 4.3g, Sugar: 2.5g, Protein: 4g, Sodium: 67mg

SIMPLE ASPARAGUS

Preparation Time: 10 minutes

Cooking Time: 2 minutes

Servings: 4

Ingredients:
- 1 pound fresh asparagus, trimmed
- 2 tablespoons olive oil
- Salt and ground black pepper, as required

Directions:
1. In the Instant Pot Duo Crisp Air Fryer pot, place 1 cup of water.
2. Arrange the "Multi-Functional Rack" in the pot.
3. Place the asparagus over the rack.
4. Cover the pot with "Pressure Lid" and seal it.
5. Select "Steam" and set the time for 2 minutes.
6. Press "Start" to begin cooking.
7. When cooking time is completed, do a "Quick" release.
8. Open the lid and transfer the asparagus onto serving plates.
9. Drizzle with oil and sprinkle with salt and black pepper.
10. Serve hot.

Nutritional Information per Serving:
Calories: 83, Fat: 7.1g, Net Carbohydrates: 2g, Carbohydrates: 4.4g, Fiber: 2.4g, Sugar: 2.1g, Protein: 2.5g, Sodium: 41mg

GLAZED CARROTS

Preparation Time: 10 minutes   Cooking Time: 12 minutes   Servings: 4

Ingredients:

- 3 cups carrots, peeled and cut into large chunks
- 1 tablespoon olive oil
- 2 tablespoons maple syrup
- 1 tablespoon fresh parsley, minced
- Salt and ground black pepper, as required
- Non-stick cooking spray

Directions:

1. Add the carrot, oil, maple syrup, thyme, salt, and black pepper to a bowl.
2. Grease the "Air Fryer Basket" with cooking spray and then arrange in the bottom of the Instant Pot Duo Crisp Air Fryer.
3. Cover the pot with "Air Fryer Lid" and seal it.
4. Select "Air Fry" and set the temperature to 390 °F for 12 minutes.
5. Press "Start" to begin preheating.
6. When the unit shows "Hot" instead of "On," open the lid and place the carrot chunks into the basket.
7. Again, cover the pot with "Air Fryer Lid" and seal it.
8. Press "Start" to begin cooking.
9. While cooking, flip the carrot chunks once halfway through.
10. When cooking time is completed, open the lid and serve hot.

Nutritional Information per Serving:

Calories: 90, Fat: 3.5g, Net Carbohydrates: 12.8g, Carbohydrates: 14.9g, Fiber: 2.1g, Sugar: 10g, Protein: 0.7g, Sodium: 97mg

JACKET POTATOES

Preparation Time: 15 minutes   Cooking Time: 20 minutes   Servings: 2

Ingredients:

- 2 potatoes
- Non-stick cooking spray
- 1 tablespoon mozzarella cheese, shredded
- 3 tablespoons sour cream
- 1 tablespoon butter, softened
- 1 teaspoon fresh chives, minced
- Salt and ground black pepper, as required

Directions:

1. With a fork, prick the potatoes.
2. Grease the "Air Fryer Basket" with cooking spray and then arrange in the pot of Instant Pot Duo Crisp Air Fryer.
3. Cover the pot with "Air Fryer Lid" and seal it.
4. Select "Air Fry" and set the temperature to 355 °F for 20 minutes.
5. Press "Start" to begin preheating.
6. When the unit shows "Hot" instead of "On," open the lid and place the potatoes into the basket.
7. Again, cover the pot with "Air Fryer Lid" and seal it.
8. Press "Start" to begin cooking.
9. Open the lid and transfer the potatoes onto a platter when cooking time is completed.
10. In a bowl, add the remaining ingredients and mix until well combined.
11. Open potatoes from the center and stuff them with cheese mixture.
12. Serve immediately.

Nutritional Information per Serving:

Calories: 277, Fat: 12.2g, Net Carbohydrates: 29.7g, Carbohydrates: 34.8g, Fiber: 5.1g, Sugar: 2.5g, Protein: 8.2g, Sodium: 226mg

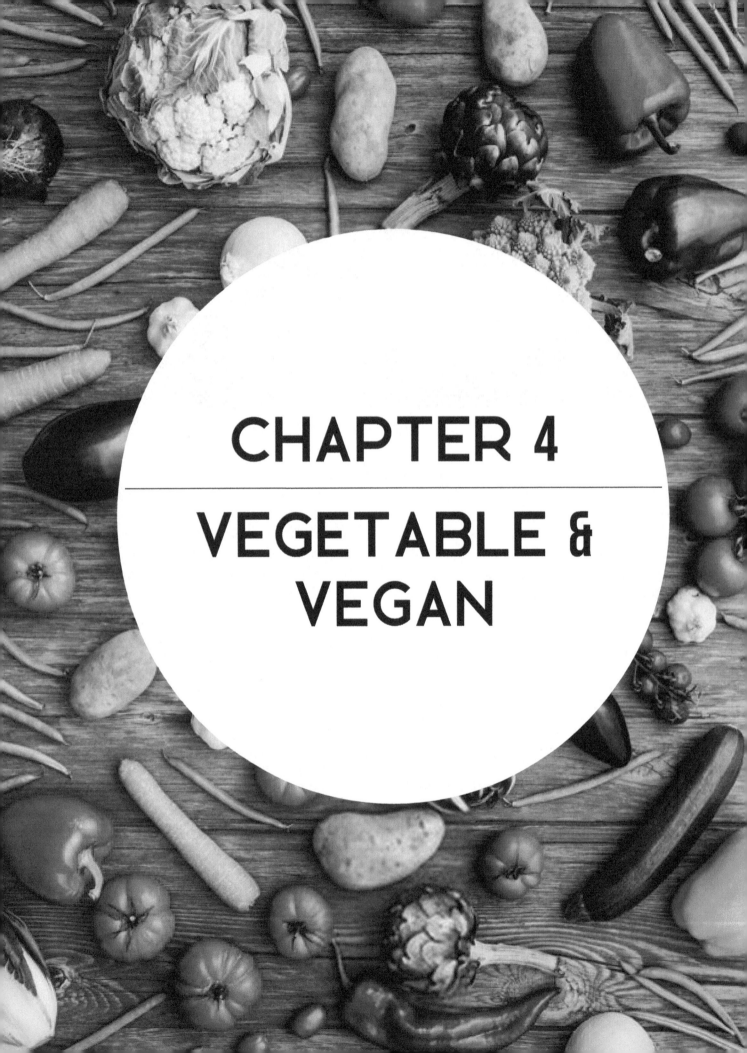

CHAPTER 4

VEGETABLE & VEGAN

SPINACH WITH COTTAGE CHEESE

Preparation Time: 15 minutes   Cooking Time: 13 minutes   Servings: 6

Ingredients:

- 1 tablespoon butter
- 1 large yellow onion, chopped
- 4 garlic cloves, minced
- 1 (1-inch) piece fresh ginger, minced
- 2 green chilies, chopped
- 1 teaspoon ground cumin
- 1 teaspoon ground coriander
- ½ teaspoon red chili powder
- ½ teaspoon ground turmeric
- Salt, as required
- 20 ounces fresh spinach, chopped
- 2 tablespoons arrowroot flour
- 10-ounce cottage cheese, cut into small pieces

Directions:

1. In the pot of Instant Pot Duo Crisp Air Fryer, place the butter and press "Sauté."
2. Press "Start" to begin cooking and heat for about 2-3 minutes.
3. Now add the onion, garlic, ginger, green chili and spices and cook for about 1 minute.
4. Add the spinach and cook for about 2 minutes.
5. Press "Cancel" to stop cooking and stir the mixture well.
6. Cover the pot with "Pressure Lid" and seal it.
7. Select "Pressure" and set the time for 4 minutes.
8. Press "Start" to begin cooking.
9. When cooking time is completed, do a "Natural" release.
10. Open the lid, and with an immersion blender, blend the mixture until smooth.
11. Press "Sauté" of the pot and place the cottage cheese into the spinach mixture.
12. Press "Start" to begin cooking and cook for about 2-3 minutes.
13. Press "Cancel" to stop cooking and serve hot.

Nutritional Information per Serving:

Calories: 100, Fat: 3.4g, Net Carbohydrates: 29.7g, Carbohydrates: 34.8g, Fiber: 5.1g, Sugar: 2.5g, Protein: 8.2g, Sodium: 312mg

RATATOUILLE

Preparation Time: 20 minutes   Cooking Time: 6 minutes   Servings: 5

Ingredients:

- 1 large zucchini, sliced into thin circles
- 1 medium eggplant, sliced into thin circles,
- 2 medium tomatoes, sliced into thin circles
- 1 small red onion, sliced into thin circles
- 1 tablespoon fresh thyme leaves, minced and divided
- Salt and ground black pepper, as required
- 2 large garlic cloves, chopped finely
- 2 tablespoons olive oil
- 1 tablespoon balsamic vinegar

Directions:

1. Add all vegetables, half of the thyme, salt, and black pepper in a bowl and toss to coat well.
2. In the bottom of a foil-lined springform pan, spread some garlic.
3. Arrange alternating slices of zucchini, eggplant, tomatoes and onion, starting at the outer edge of the pan towards the center, overlapping the slices slightly.
4. Sprinkle with the remaining garlic, thyme, salt and black pepper.
5. Drizzle with oil and vinegar evenly.
6. In the Instant Pot Duo Crisp Air Fryer pot, place 1 cup of water.
7. Arrange the "Multi-Functional Rack" in the pot.
8. Place springform pan over the rack.
9. Cover the pot with "Pressure Lid" and seal it.
10. Select "Pressure" and set the time for 6 minutes.
11. Press "Start" to begin cooking.
12. When cooking time is completed, do a "Natural" release.
13. Open the lid and serve hot.

Nutritional Information per Serving:

Calories: 96, Fat: 6g, Net Carbohydrates: 5.9g, Carbohydrates: 10.7g, Fiber: 4.8g, Sugar: 5.3g, Protein: 2.1g, Sodium: 40mg

VEGGIE CASSEROLE

Preparation Time: 15 minutes   Cooking Time: 4½ hours   Servings: 6

Ingredients:

- 1 tablespoon unsalted butter, melted
- 4 medium zucchinis, peeled and sliced in rounds
- 1 green bell pepper, seeded and sliced into strips
- 2 cups fresh tomatoes, chopped finely
- 1 white onion, sliced thinly
- 1 tablespoon fresh thyme, minced
- 1 tablespoon fresh rosemary, minced
- Salt and ground black pepper, as required
- ½ cup Parmesan cheese, grated

Directions:

1. In the pot of Instant Pot Duo Crisp Air Fryer, add all ingredients except for cheese and mix well.
2. Cover the pot with "Air Fryer Lid" and seal it.
3. Select "Slow Cook" and set the time for 3 hours.
4. Press "Start" to begin cooking.
5. Open the lid and evenly sprinkle the top with the cheese when cooking time is completed.
6. Again, Cover the pot with "Air Fryer Lid" and seal it.
7. Select "Slow Cook" and set the time for 1½ hours.
8. Press "Start" to begin cooking.
9. When cooking time is completed, open the lid and serve hot.

Nutritional Information per Serving:
Calories: 89, Fat: 14.1g, Net Carbohydrates: 7.4g, Carbohydrates: 10.6g, Fiber: 3.2g, Sugar: 5.6g, Protein: 5.3g, Sodium: 116mg

MARINATED TOFU

Preparation Time: 15 minutes   Cooking Time: 25 minutes   Servings: 3

Ingredients:

- 2 tablespoon soy sauce
- 2 tablespoon fish sauce
- 1 teaspoon olive oil
- 12 ounces extra-firm tofu, drained and cubed into 1-inch size
- Non-stick cooking spray
- 1 tablespoon scallion greens, chopped
- ½ teaspoon sesame seeds

Directions:

1. Add the soy sauce, fish sauce, and oil to a large bowl and mix until well combined.
2. Add the tofu cubes and toss to coat well.
3. Set aside to marinate for about 30 minutes, tossing occasionally.
4. Grease the "Air Fryer Basket" with cooking spray and then arrange in the pot of Instant Pot Duo Crisp Air Fryer.
5. Cover the pot with "Air Fryer Lid" and seal it.
6. Select "Air Fry" and set the temperature to 355 °F for 25 minutes.
7. Press "Start" to begin preheating.
8. When the unit shows "Hot" instead of "On," open the lid and place the tofu cubes into the basket.
9. Again, cover the pot with "Air Fryer Lid" and seal it.
10. Press "Start" to begin cooking.
11. While cooking, flip the tofu after every 10 minutes.
12. When cooking time is completed, open the lid and serve hot with the garnishing of scallion greens and sesame seeds.

Nutritional Information per Serving:

Calories: 130, Fat: 8.4g, Net Carbohydrates: 3.1g, Carbohydrates: 3.8g, Fiber: 0.7g, Sugar: 1.2g, Protein: 12.6g, Sodium: 1200mg

CHAPTER 5

FISH & SEAFOOD

PESTO SALMON

Preparation Time: 10 minutes   Cooking Time: 20 minutes   Servings: 4

Ingredients:
- 4 (6-ounce) salmon fillet
- 2 teaspoons olive oil
- Pinch of salt
- Non-stick cooking spray
- ½ cup pesto

Directions:
1. Drizzle the salmon fillets with oil evenly and sprinkle with a pinch of salt.
2. Grease the "Air Fryer Basket" with cooking spray and then arrange in the bottom of the Instant Pot Duo Crisp Air Fryer.
3. Cover the pot with "Air Fryer Lid" and seal it.
4. Select "Air Fry" and set the temperature to 270 °F for 20 minutes.
5. Press "Start" to begin preheating.
6. When the unit shows "Hot" instead of "On," open the lid and place the salmon fillets into the basket.
7. Again, cover the pot with "Air Fryer Lid" and seal it.
8. Press "Start" to begin cooking.
9. Open the lid and place the salmon fillets onto a platter when cooking time is completed.
10. Top with the pesto and serve immediately.

Nutritional Information per Serving:
Calories: 380, Fat: 25.8g, Net Carbohydrates: 1.5g, Carbohydrates: 2g, Fiber: 0.5g, Sugar: 2g, Protein: 36g, Sodium: 304mg

Preparation Time: 5 minutes

Cooking Time: 5 minutes

Servings: 2

Ingredients:

- ¼ teaspoon garam masala powder
- ¼ teaspoon ground cumin
- ¼ teaspoon ground coriander
- ¼ teaspoon ground turmeric
- Salt and ground black pepper, as required
- 2 (5-ounce) trout fillets

Directions:

1. In a bowl, mix the spices.
2. In the Instant Pot Duo Crisp Air Fryer pot, place 1 cup of water.
3. Arrange the "Multi-Functional Rack" in the pot.
4. Place the trout fillets over the rack.
5. Cover the pot with "Pressure Lid" and seal it.
6. Select "Steam" and set the time for 5 minutes.
7. Press "Start" to begin cooking.
8. When cooking time is completed, do a "Quick" release.
9. Open the lid and serve immediately.

Nutritional Information per Serving:

Calories: 371, Fat: 12.1g, Net Carbohydrates: 0.2g, Carbohydrates: 0.3g, Fiber: 0.1g, Sugar: 0g, Protein: 37.8g, Sodium: 174mg

CREAMY LOBSTER TAILS

Preparation Time: 15 minutes   Cooking Time: 3 minutes   Servings: 3

Ingredients:

- 1 teaspoon old bay seasoning
- 2 pounds fresh lobster tails
- 1 scallion, chopped
- ½ cup mayonnaise
- 2 tablespoons unsalted butter, melted
- 2 tablespoons fresh lemon juice, divided

Directions:

1. In the pot of Instant Pot Duo Crisp Air Fryer, place 1½ cps of water and 1-2 pinches of old bay seasoning.
2. Arrange the "Multi-Functional Rack" in the pot.
3. Arrange the lobster tail over the rack, shell side down, meat side up.
4. Drizzle the lobster tails with 1 tablespoon of lemon juice.
5. Cover the pot with "Pressure Lid" and seal it.
6. Select "Pressure" and set the time for 3 minutes.
7. Press "Start" to begin cooking.
8. When cooking time is completed, do a "Quick" release.
9. Open the lid and transfer the tails into the ice bath bowl for about 1 minute.
10. With kitchen shears, cut the underbelly of the tail down the center.
11. Remove the meat and chop it up into large chunks.
12. Add the lobster meat, scallions, mayonnaise, butter, seasoning, and lemon juice in a large bowl and mix well.
13. Refrigerate for at least 15 minutes before serving.

Nutritional Information per Serving:

Calories: 582, Fat: 36.9g, Net Carbohydrates: 0.4g, Carbohydrates: 0.6g, Fiber: 0.2g, Sugar: 0.3g, Protein: 57.7g, Sodium: 1090mg

VANILLA SHRIMP

Preparation Time: 15 minutes   Cooking Time: 30 minutes   Servings: 3

Ingredients:

- 1 vanilla bean
- 12 large shrimp, peeled and deveined
- ¼ teaspoon paprika
- Salt and ground black pepper, as required

Directions:

1. Split the vanilla bean and scrape out the seeds.
2. Add the vanilla ban seeds and remaining ingredients in a bowl and mix until well combined.
3. Fill the Instant Pot Duo Crisp Air Fryer pot with water up to the ½-full mark.
4. Select "Sous Vide" and set the temperature to 136 °F for 30 minutes.
5. Cover the pot with "Pressure Lid" and seal it.
6. Press "Start" to begin preheating.
7. Meanwhile, split the vanilla bean in half and scrape out the seeds.
8. In a bowl, add shrimp, vanilla seeds, paprika, salt and pepper and toss to coat.
9. In a cooking pouch, place the shrimp mixture.
10. Seal the pouch tightly after squeezing out the excess air.
11. When the unit shows "Hot" instead of "On," open the lid and place the pouch in the pot.
12. Again, cover the pot with "Pressure Lid" and seal it.
13. Press "Start" to begin cooking.
14. Open the lid and remove the pouch from the inner pot when the cooking time is completed.
15. Carefully open the pouch and transfer the shrimp with cooking liquid into a serving bowl.
16. Serve hot.

Nutritional Information per Serving:

Calories: 106, Fat: 1.5g, Net Carbohydrates: 1.3g, Carbohydrates: 1.4g, Fiber: 0.1g, Sugar: 0g, Protein: 20.1g, Sodium: 265mg

CHAPTER 6

BEEF, PORK & LAMB

BACON-WRAPPED FILET MIGNON

Preparation Time: 10 minutes

Cooking Time: 15 minutes

Servings: 2

Ingredients:

- 2 bacon slices
- 2 (6-ounces) filet mignon
- Ground black pepper, as required
- 1 teaspoon avocado oil
- Non-stick cooking spray

Directions:

1. Wrap 1 bacon slice around each filet and secure with a toothpick.
2. Season each filet evenly with black pepper and then coat with avocado oil.
3. Grease the "Air Fryer Basket" with cooking spray and then arrange in the pot of Instant Pot Duo Crisp Air Fryer.
4. Cover the pot with "Air Fryer Lid" and seal it.
5. Select "Air Fry" and set the temperature to 375 °F for 15 minutes.
6. Press "Start" to begin preheating.
7. When the unit shows "Hot" instead of "On," open the lid and place the filets into the basket.
8. Again, cover the pot with "Air Fryer Lid" and seal it.
9. Press "Start" to begin cooking.
10. While cooking, flip the filets once halfway through.
11. When cooking time is completed, open the lid and serve hot.

Nutritional Information per Serving:

Calories: 464, Fat: 23.6g, Net Carbohydrates: 0.4g, Carbohydrates: 0.5g, Fiber: 0.1g, Sugar: 0g, Protein: 58.5g, Sodium: 838mg

BEEF JERKY

Preparation Time: 10 minutes

Cooking Time: 7 hours

Servings: 6

Ingredients:

- ¼ cup low-sodium soy sauce
- 2 tablespoons Worcestershire sauce
- 2 tablespoons brown sugar
- Salt, as required
- 1½ pounds beef eye of round, cut in ¼-inch slices

Directions:

1. Add all the ingredients except for beef and beat until sugar is dissolved in a bowl.
2. In a large resealable plastic bag, place the beef slices and marinade.
3. Seal the bag and rub to coat.
4. Refrigerate to marinate overnight.
5. Remove from the refrigerator and strain the beef slices discarding the marinade.
6. Place the beef slices into the "Dehydrating Tray" in a single layer.
7. Arrange the tray in the pot of Instant Pot Duo Crisp Air Fryer.
8. Cover the pot with "Air Fryer Lid" and seal it.
9. Select "Dehydrate" and set the temperature to 155 °F for 7 hours.
10. Press "Start" to begin cooking.
11. Open the lid and transfer the beef jerky onto a platter when cooking time is completed.
12. Set aside to cool before serving.

Nutritional Information per Serving:

Calories: 230, Fat: 7.1g, Net Carbohydrates: 4.6g, Carbohydrates: 4.6g, Fiber: 0g, Sugar: 4.6g, Protein: 35.1g, Sodium: 744mg

SIMPLE PORK CHOPS

Preparation Time: 10 minutes   Cooking Time: 12 minutes   Servings: 2

Ingredients:

- 2 (6-ounce) (½-inch thick) pork chops
- ¼ teaspoon dried basil, crushed
- Salt and ground black pepper, as required
- Non-stick cooking spray

Directions:

1. Season the pork chops with basil, salt and black pepper evenly.
2. Grease the "Broiling Tray" with cooking spray and then arrange in the bottom of the Instant Pot Duo Crisp Air Fryer.
3. Cover the pot with "Air Fryer Lid" and seal it.
4. Select "Broil" and set the time for 18 minutes.
5. Press "Start" to begin preheating.
6. When the unit shows "Hot" instead of "On," open the lid and place the chops onto the tray.
7. Again, cover the pot with "Air Fryer Lid" and seal it.
8. Press "Start" to begin cooking.
9. While cooking, flip the chops once after 12 minutes.
10. When cooking time is completed, open the lid and serve hot.

Nutritional Information per Serving:

Calories: 544, Fat: 42.3g, Net Carbohydrates: 0g, Carbohydrates: 0.g, Fiber: 0g, Sugar: 0g, Protein: 38.2g, Sodium: 197mg

BRAISED LAMB SHANKS

Preparation Time: 10 minutes

Cooking Time: 45 minutes

Servings: 2

Ingredients:

- 2 pounds lamb shanks, trimmed
- Salt and ground black pepper, as required
- 1 tablespoon olive oil
- 10 whole garlic cloves, peeled
- 1 cup chicken broth

- 1 tablespoon tomato paste
- ½ teaspoon dried rosemary, crushed
- 2 tablespoons fresh lemon juice
- 1 tablespoon unsalted butter

Directions:

1. Season the shanks with salt and black pepper evenly.
2. In the pot of Instant Pot Duo Crisp Air Fryer, place the oil and press "Sauté."
3. Press "Start" to begin cooking and heat for about 2-3 minutes.
4. Add the shanks and sear for about 2-3 minutes per side or until browned completely.
5. Add the garlic cloves and cook for about 1 minute.
6. Press "Cancel" to stop cooking and stir in the remaining ingredients.
7. Cover the pot with "Pressure Lid" and seal it.
8. Select "Pressure" and set the time for 30 minutes.
9. Press "Start" to begin cooking.
10. When cooking time is completed, do a "Natural" release.
11. Open the lid, and with tongs, transfer the lamb shanks onto a platter.
12. Press "Sauté" of the pot and then press "Start" to begin cooking.
13. Cook for about 5 minutes.
14. Add in the lemon juice and butter and stir until smooth.
15. Press "Cancel" to stop cooking and pour sauce over shanks.
16. Serve immediately.

Nutritional Information per Serving:

Calories: 980, Fat: 44g, Net Carbohydrates: 5.2g, Carbohydrates: 6g, Fiber: 0.8g, Sugar: 1.8g, Protein: 13.7g, Sodium: 813mg

CHAPTER 7
POULTRY

SPINACH STUFFED CHICKEN BREASTS

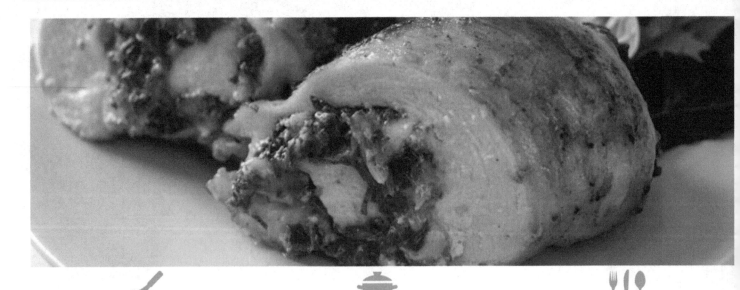

Preparation Time: 15 minutes   Cooking Time: 33 minutes   Servings: 2

Ingredients:

- 1 tablespoon olive oil
- 1¾ ounces fresh spinach
- ¼ cup ricotta cheese, shredded
- 2 (4-ounce) skinless, boneless chicken breasts
- Salt and ground black pepper, as required
- 2 tablespoons cheddar cheese, grated
- ¼ teaspoon paprika
- Non-stick cooking spray

Directions:

1. In the pot of Instant Pot Duo Crisp Air Fryer, place the oil and press "Sauté."
2. Press "Start" to begin cooking and heat for about 2-3 minutes.
3. Now add the spinach and cook for about 3-4 minutes.
4. Stir in the ricotta and cook for about 40-60 seconds.
5. Press "Cancel" to stop cooking and transfer the spinach mixture into a bowl. Set aside to cool.
6. Cut slits into the chicken breasts about ¼-inch apart but not all the way through.
7. Stuff each chicken breast with the spinach mixture.
8. Sprinkle each chicken breast with salt and black pepper, cheddar cheese and paprika.
9. Grease the "Air Fryer Basket" with cooking spray and then arrange in the bottom of the Instant Pot Duo Crisp Air Fryer.
10. Cover the pot with "Air Fryer Lid" and seal it.
11. Select "Air Fry" and set the temperature to 390 °F for 25 minutes.
12. Press "Start" to begin preheating.
13. When the unit shows "Hot" instead of "On," open the lid and place the chicken breasts into the basket.
14. Again, cover the pot with "Air Fryer Lid" and seal it.
15. Press "Start" to begin cooking.
16. When cooking time is completed, open the lid and serve hot.

Nutritional Information per Serving:

Calories: 279, Fat: 16g, Net Carbohydrates: 2g, Carbohydrates: 2.7g, Fiber: 0.7g, Sugar: 0.3g, Protein: 31.4g, Sodium: 220mg

BUTTER CHICKEN

Preparation Time: 15 minutes

Cooking Time: 12 minutes

Servings: 8

Ingredients:

- ½ cup butter, cubed and divided
- 1 large yellow onion, chopped finely
- 6 garlic cloves, minced
- 2 tablespoons fresh ginger, minced
- 3 pounds boneless, skinless chicken breasts, cubed
- 1 cup tomato sauce

- 3 tablespoons tomato paste
- 1½ tablespoons garam masala powder
- 1 teaspoon ground turmeric
- 1 teaspoon kosher salt
- 2/3 cup chicken broth
- 2/3 cup heavy cream
- ¼ cup fresh cilantro, chopped

Directions:

1. In the pot of Instant Pot Duo Crisp Air Fryer, place the 2 tablespoons of the butter and press "Sauté."
2. Press "Start" to begin cooking and heat for about 2-3 minutes.
3. Now add the onion, garlic and ginger and cook for about 2 minutes.
4. Press "Cancel" to stop cooking and stir in the remaining ingredients except for the cream and cilantro.
5. Cover the pot with "Pressure Lid" and seal it.
6. Select "Pressure" and set the time for 5 minutes.
7. Press "Start" to begin cooking.
8. When cooking time is completed, do a "Quick" release.
9. Open the lid and press "Sauté" of the pot.
10. Press "Start" to begin cooking.
11. Stir in the remaining butter and heavy cream and cook for about 2 minutes.
12. Press "Cancel" to stop cooking and serve hot with the garnishing of cilantro.

Nutritional Information per Serving:

Calories: 492. Fat: 28.2g, Net Carbohydrates: 5.4g, Carbohydrates: 6.8g, Fiber: 1.4g, Sugar: 3g, Protein: 51.1g, Sodium: 757mg

GLAZED TURKEY BREAST

Preparation Time: 10 minutes

Cooking Time: 55 minutes

Servings: 10

Ingredients:

- 1 (5-pound) boneless turkey breast
- Salt and ground black pepper, as required
- Non-stick cooking spray
- 3 tablespoons honey
- 2 tablespoon Dijon mustard
- 1 tablespoon butter, softened

Directions:

1. Season the turkey breast with salt and black pepper generously and spray with cooking spray.
2. Grease the "Air Fryer Basket" with cooking spray and then arrange in the bottom of the Instant Pot Duo Crisp Air Fryer.
3. Cover the pot with "Air Fryer Lid" and seal it.
4. Select "Air Fry" and set the temperature to 350 °F for 55 minutes.
5. Press "Start" to begin preheating.
6. When the unit shows "Hot" instead of "On," open the lid and place the turkey breast into the basket.
7. Again, cover the pot with "Air Fryer Lid" and seal it.
8. Press "Start" to begin cooking.
9. Meanwhile, mix the maple syrup, mustard, and butter for glaze in a bowl.
10. While cooking, flip the turkey breast twice, first after 25 minutes and then after 37 minutes.
11. After 50 minutes of cooking, coat the turkey breast with the glaze.
12. When cooking time is completed, open the lid and place the turkey onto a cutting board for about 5 minutes before slicing.
13. Cut into desired-sized slices and serve.

Nutritional Information per Serving:

Calories: 252, Fat: 2.5g, Net Carbohydrates: 5.3g, Carbohydrates: 5.4g, Fiber: 0.1g, Sugar: 5.2g, Protein: 56.4g, Sodium: 170mg

BUTTERED DUCK LEGS

Preparation Time: 10 minutes   Cooking Time: 6 hours   Servings: 4

Ingredients:

- 4 duck legs
- Salt and ground black pepper, as required
- ¼ cup butter, melted

Directions:

1. Season the duck legs with salt and black pepper generously.
2. In a baking dish, arrange the duck legs in a single layer and refrigerate, covered overnight
3. Place the butter evenly in the Instant Pot Duo Crisp Air Fryer pot.
4. Arrange the duck legs over oil in a single layer.
5. Cover the pot with "Air Fryer Lid" and seal it.
6. Select "Slow Cook" and set the time for 6 hours.
7. Press "Start" to begin cooking.
8. When cooking time is completed, open the lid and serve hot.

Nutritional Information per Serving:

Calories: 531   Carbohydrates: 0g   Protein: 70.2g
Fat: 25.9g   Fiber: 0g   Sodium: 381mg
Net Carbohydrates: 0g   Sugar: 0g

CHAPTER 8

SOUP & STEW

TOMATO SOUP

Preparation Time: 10 minutes   Cooking Time: 20 minutes   Servings: 4

Ingredients:

- 4 cups fresh tomatoes, cored and halved
- ½ of onion, chopped
- 1/3 cup fresh basil, chopped and divided
- 2 garlic cloves, minced
- Salt and ground black pepper, as required
- 5 tablespoons extra-virgin olive oil
- 5 tablespoons crème fraiche

Directions:

1. Fill the Instant Pot Duo Crisp Air Fryer pot with water up to the ½-full mark.
2. Select "Sous Vide" and set the temperature to 176 °F for 20 minutes.
3. Cover the pot with "Pressure Lid" and seal it.
4. Press "Start" to begin preheating.
5. Meanwhile, place the tomatoes, onion, ¼ cup of basil and garlic in a cooking pouch.
6. Seal the pouch tightly after squeezing out the excess air.
7. When the unit shows "Hot" instead of "On," open the lid and place the pouch in the pot.
8. Again, cover the pot with "Pressure Lid" and seal it.
9. Press "Start" to begin cooking.
10. Open the lid and remove the pouch from the inner pot when the cooking time is completed.
11. Carefully open the pouch and transfer the tomato mixture into a blender.
12. Add olive oil, crème fraiche, salt and pepper and pulse until smooth.
13. Serve immediately with the garnishing of the remaining basil.

Nutritional Information per Serving:

Calories: 255, Fat: 24.8g, Net Carbohydrates: 6.9g, Carbohydrates: 9.4g, Fiber: 2.5g, Sugar: 5.4g, Protein: 2.3g, Sodium: 56mg

BARLEY & BEANS SOUP

Preparation Time: 15 minutes   Cooking Time: 8 hours 5 mins   Servings: 10

Ingredients:

- ½ cup pearl barley
- 1 cup dried Great Northern beans, rinsed
- 2 medium carrots, peeled and chopped
- 1 small onion, chopped
- 2 celery stalks, chopped
- 4 garlic cloves, minced
- 2 teaspoons mixed dried herbs (basil, thyme, marjoram, oregano), crushed
- 1 (14-ounce) can whole tomatoes with juice, chopped
- Salt and ground black pepper, as required
- 6 cups water
- ¼ cup Parmesan cheese, grated
- 3 cups fresh spinach, chopped
- 2 tablespoons olive oil

Directions:

1. In the Instant Pot Duo Crisp Air Fryer pot, place all ingredients except for spinach and stir to combine.
2. Cover the pot with "Air Fryer Lid" and seal it.
3. Select "Slow Cook" and set the time for 8 hours.
4. Press "Start" to begin cooking.
5. Open the lid and stir in the spinach and cheese when cooking time is completed.
6. Immediately cover the pot with "Air Fryer Lid" and seal it.
7. Select "Slow Cook" and set the time for 10 minutes.
8. Press "Start" to begin cooking.
9. When cooking time is completed, open the lid and serve hot with the drizzling of oil.

Nutritional Information per Serving:

Calories: 179, Fat: 3.7g, Net Carbohydrates: 14.7g, Carbohydrates: 26.1g, Fiber: 11.4g, Sugar: 5.2g, Protein: 11.7g, Sodium: 428mg

PORK & VEGGIE STEW

Preparation Time: 15 minutes   Cooking Time: 1 hour   Servings: 8

Ingredients:

- 1 tablespoon coconut oil
- ¼ pound shiitake mushrooms, stems removed and halved
- ¼ cup shallots, sliced thinly
- 4 garlic cloves, smashed
- 1 tablespoon fresh ginger, sliced

- 3 pounds pork shoulder, cubed into 2-inch size
- 3 tablespoons fish sauce
- 1 cup chicken broth
- 3 carrots, peeled and cut into ½-inch slices diagonally
- ½ cup fresh cilantro, chopped

Directions:

1. In the pot of Instant Pot Duo Crisp, place the oil and press "Sauté."
2. Press "Start" to begin cooking and heat for about 2-3 minutes.
3. Now add the mushrooms and shallots and cook for about 3-5 minutes.
4. Stir in the garlic and ginger and cook for about 1 minute.
5. Add the pork cubes and cook for about 1-2 minutes.
6. Press "Cancel" to stop cooking and stir in the fish sauce and broth.
7. Cover the pot with "Pressure Lid" and seal it.
8. Select "Pressure" and set the time for 40 minutes.
9. Press "Start" to begin cooking.
10. When cooking time is completed, do a "Natural" release.
11. Open the lid and transfer the pork cubes into a bowl with a slotted spoon.
12. In the pot, add the carrots and stir to combine.
13. Cover the pot with "Pressure Lid" and seal it.
14. Select "Pressure" and set it to "High" for 10 minutes.
15. Press "Start" to begin cooking.
16. When cooking time is completed, do a "Quick" release.
17. Open the lid and stir in the pork cubes and cilantro.
18. Serve hot.

Nutritional Information per Serving:

Calories: 547, Fat: 38.4g, Net Carbohydrates: 5.2g, Carbohydrates: 6.2g, Fiber: 1g, Sugar: 1.8g, Protein: 42.4g, Sodium: 821mg

HERBED SEAFOOD STEW

Preparation Time: 20 minutes   Cooking Time: 4¾ hours   Servings: 8

Ingredients:

- 1 celery stalk, chopped
- 1 yellow onion, chopped
- 3 garlic cloves, chopped
- 1 cup fresh cilantro leaves, chopped
- 1 cup tomatoes, chopped finely
- 4 cups chicken broth
- 2 tablespoons fresh lemon juice
- 2 tablespoons olive oil

- 3 teaspoons mixed dried herbs (rosemary, thyme, marjoram)
- Salt and ground black pepper, as required
- 1 pound cod fillets, cubed
- 1 pound shrimp, peeled and deveined
- 1 pound scallops
- ¾ cup crabmeat

Directions:

1. In the pot of Instant Pot Duo Crisp Air Fryer, add all ingredients except for seafood and mix well.
2. Cover the pot with "Air Fryer Lid" and seal it.
3. Select "Slow Cook" and set the time for 4 hours.
4. Press "Start" to begin cooking.
5. Open the lid and stir in the seafood when cooking time is completed.
6. Again, cover the pot with "Air Fryer Lid" and seal it.
7. Select "Slow Cook" and set the time for 45 minutes.
8. Press "Start" to begin cooking.
9. When cooking time is completed, open the lid and serve hot.

Nutritional Information per Serving:

Calories: 228, Fat: 6.3g, Net Carbohydrates: 00g, Carbohydrates: 5.6g, Fiber: 0.8g, Sugar: 1.7g, Protein: 35.8g, Sodium: 688mg

CHAPTER 9
PASTA & RICE

CHILI MAC N' CHEESE

Preparation Time: 10 minutes

Cooking Time: 4 minutes

Servings: 6

Ingredients:

- 2 (14-ounce) cans of spicy chili
- 1 (12-ounce) can beer
- ½ cup water
- 2 cups elbow macaroni
- ½ cup hot cashew milk

Directions:

1. In the pot of Instant Pot Duo Crisp Air Fryer, place all the ingredients except for milk and stir to combine
2. Cover the pot with "Pressure Lid" and seal it.
3. Select "Pressure" and set the time for 4 minutes.
4. Press "Start" to begin cooking.
5. When cooking time is completed, do a "Quick" release.
6. Open the lid and stir in the cashew milk.
7. Serve immediately.

Nutritional Information per Serving:

Calories: 310, Fat: 6.4g, Net Carbohydrates: 39.8g, Carbohydrates: 45.3g, Fiber: 5.5g, Sugar: 3.9g, Protein: 13.5g, Sodium: 452mg

TUNA & PASTA CASSEROLE

Preparation Time: 20 minutes

Cooking Time: 4 hours

Servings: 6

Ingredients:

- Non-stick cooking spray
- 16 ounces water-packed tuna
- 10 ounces frozen mixed vegetables, thawed
- 20 ounces cream of mushroom soup
- 1 cup milk
- 2 tablespoons dried parsley flakes, crushed
- Salt and ground black pepper, as required
- 10 ounces cooked pasta (of your choice)
- ¼ cup almonds, toasted and sliced

Directions:

1. Grease the pot of Instant Pot Duo Crisp Air Fryer with cooking spray.
2. Place tuna, vegetables, mushroom soup, milk, parsley, salt, and black pepper in the prepared pot and mix well.
3. Gently fold in the cooked pasta and sprinkle with almonds evenly.
4. Cover the pot with "Air Fryer Lid" and seal it.
5. Press "Slow Cook" and set the time for 4 hours.
6. Press "Start" to begin cooking.
7. When cooking time is completed, open the lid and serve warm.

Nutritional Information per Serving:

Calories: 267, Fat: 7.2g, Net Carbohydrates: 20.9g, Carbohydrates: 24.1g, Fiber: 3.2g, Sugar: 4. 4g, Protein: 25.8g, Sodium: 404mg

ASPARAGUS RISOTTO

Preparation Time: 15 minutes   Cooking Time: 15 minutes   Servings: 8

Ingredients:

- 2 tablespoons unsalted butter
- 2 cups onion, chopped finely
- 2 cups Arborio rice
- 1½ cups asparagus, tough ends removed and cut into 1-inch chunks
- 1 cup cherry tomatoes
- 3 garlic cloves, minced
- 3 cups chicken broth
- 2 tablespoons fresh lemon juice
- 1 teaspoon dried oregano
- Salt, as required
- 2/3 cup Parmesan cheese, shredded

Directions:

1. In the pot of Instant Pot Duo Crisp Air Fryer, place the butter and press "Sauté."
2. Press "Start" to begin cooking and heat for about 2-3 minutes.
3. Now add the onion and cook for about 3 minutes.
4. Stir in the rice and cook for about 3 minutes.
5. Press "Cancel" to stop cooking and stir in the veggies, broth, lemon juice, oregano and salt.
6. Cover the pot with "Pressure Lid" and seal it.
7. Select "Pressure" and set the time for 6 minutes.
8. Press "Start" to begin cooking.
9. When cooking time is completed, do a "Quick" release.
10. Open the lid and stir in the Parmesan cheese.
11. Serve warm.

Nutritional Information per Serving:

Calories: 267, Fat: 6g, Net Carbohydrates: 00g, Carbohydrates: 43.6g, Fiber: 2.8g, Sugar: 2.4g, Protein: 8.9g, Sodium: 243mg

RICE WITH CHICKEN & BROCCOLI

Preparation Time: 15 minutes   Cooking Time: 15 minutes   Servings: 6

Ingredients:

- 3 tablespoons dried parsley, crushed
- 1 tablespoon onion powder
- 1 tablespoon garlic powder
- ½ teaspoon red chili powder
- ½ teaspoon paprika
- 2 pounds boneless, skinless chicken breasts, sliced

- 3 cups instant white rice
- ¾ cup cream soup
- 3 cups small broccoli florets
- 1/3 cup butter
- 3 cups water

Directions:

1. In a large bowl, mix the parsley and spices.
2. Add the chicken slices and coat with spice mixture generously.
3. Arrange 6 large pieces of foil onto a smooth surface.
4. Place ½ cup of rice over each foil piece, followed by 1/6 of chicken, 2 tablespoons of cream soup, ½ cup of broccoli, 1 tablespoon of butter, and ½ cup of water.
5. Fold each foil tightly to seal the rice mixture.
6. Arrange the "Air Fryer Basket" in the pot of Instant Pot Duo Crisp.
7. Cover the pot with "Air Fryer Lid" and seal it.
8. Select "Air Fry" and set the temperature to 390 °F for 15 minutes.
9. Press "Start" to begin preheating.
10. When the unit shows "Hot" instead of "On," open the lid and place the foil packets into the basket.
11. Again, cover the pot with "Air Fryer Lid" and seal it.
12. Press "Start" to begin cooking.
13. When cooking time is completed, open the lid and serve hot.

Nutritional Information per Serving:

Calories: 597, Fat: 23g, Net Carbohydrates: 00g, Carbohydrates: 45.4g, Fiber: 2.5g, Sugar: 1.8g, Protein: 49.6g, Sodium: 327mg

CHAPTER 10

SNACKS

CARAMELIZED ALMONDS

Preparation Time: 10 minutes

Cooking Time: 20 minutes

Servings: 6

Ingredients:

- 1½ cups almonds
- 2 tablespoons egg white
- 2 tablespoons powdered sugar
- ½ tablespoon ground cinnamon
- Pinch of cayenne pepper
- Non-stick cooking spray

Directions:

1. In a bowl, add all the ingredients and toss to coat well.
2. Grease the "Air Fryer Basket" with cooking spray and then arrange in the pot of Instant Pot Duo Crisp Air Fryer.
3. Cover the pot with "Air Fryer Lid" and seal it.
4. Select "Air Fry" and set the temperature to 320 °F for 20 minutes.
5. Press "Start" to begin preheating.
6. When the unit shows "Hot" instead of "On," open the lid and place the almonds into the basket.
7. Again, cover the pot with "Air Fryer Lid" and seal it.
8. Press "Start" to begin cooking.
9. While cooking, stir the almonds once halfway through.
10. Open the lid and transfer the almonds into a bowl when cooking time is completed.
11. Set aside to cool before serving.

Nutritional Information per Serving:

Calories: 152, Fat: 11.9g, Net Carbohydrates: 5g, Carbohydrates: 8.3g, Fiber: 3.3g, Sugar: 3.7g, Protein: 5.6g, Sodium: 5mg

CANDIED LEMON PEEL

Preparation Time: 15 minutes

Cooking Time: 18 minutes

Servings: 40

Ingredients:

- 1 pound lemons
- 5 cups water, divided
- 2¼ cups white sugar, divided

Directions:

1. Slice the lemon in half lengthwise and extract the juice. Discard the juice.
2. Slice each half in quarters, and with a melon-baller, remove the pulp. Cut the lemon quarters into thin strips.
3. In the Instant Pot Duo Crisp Air Fryer pot, place the lemon peel strips and 4 cups of water.
4. Cover the pot with "Pressure Lid" and seal it.
5. Select "Pressure" and set the time for 3 minutes.
6. Press "Start" to begin cooking.
7. When cooking time is completed, do a "Natural" release.
8. Open the lid and strain the lemon peel strips.
9. Rinse the strips completely.
10. Remove water from the pot, and with paper towels, pat dry it.
11. In the Instant Pot Duo Crisp Air Fryer pot, place the lemon peel strips, 1 cup of sugar, and 1 cup of water and press "Sauté."
12. Press "Start" to begin cooking and cook for about 5 minutes.
13. Press "Cancel" to stop cooking and stir the mixture well.
14. Cover the pot with "Pressure Lid" and seal it.
15. Select "Pressure" and set the time for 10 minutes.
16. Press "Start" to begin cooking.
17. When cooking time is completed, do a "Natural" release.
18. Open the lid and strain the peel strips.
19. Spread the peel strips onto a cutting board for about 15-20 minutes.
20. Coat the lemon strips with remaining sugar, shaking off the excess.
21. Arrange the lemon strips onto a sheet pan and refrigerate, uncovered for at least 4 hours or overnight before serving.

Nutritional Information per Serving:

Calories: 36, Fat: 0g, Net Carbohydrates: 00g, Carbohydrates: 9.9g, Fiber: 0.3g, Sugar: 9.2g, Protein: 1g, Sodium: 1mg

PARMESAN CHICKEN WINGS

Preparation Time: 15 minutes   Cooking Time: 10 minutes   Servings: 8

Ingredients:
- 1 (3-pound) bag frozen chicken wings
- 1 cup Parmesan cheese, shredded
- ½ cup unsalted butter, melted
- 2 tablespoons ranch dressing seasoning mix
- 1 teaspoon garlic powder

Directions:
1. In the Instant Pot Duo Crisp Air Fryer pot, place 1 cup of water.
2. Arrange the "Air Fryer Basket" in the pot.
3. Place chicken wings in the "Air Fryer Basket."
4. Cover the pot with "Pressure Lid" and seal it.
5. Select "Pressure" and set the time for 5 minutes.
6. Press "Start" to begin cooking.
7. Meanwhile, add the remaining ingredients to a bowl and mix until well combined.
8. When cooking time is completed, do a "Quick" release.
9. Open the lid and top the wings with Parmesan mixture.
10. Cover the pot with "Air Fryer Lid" and seal it.
11. Select "Broil" and set the time for 6 minutes.
12. Press "Start" to begin cooking.
13. When cooking time is completed, open the lid and serve hot with the sprinkling of red pepper flakes.

Nutritional Information per Serving:
Calories: 277, Fat: 2.5g, Net Carbohydrates: 4.3g, Carbohydrates: 4.6g, Fiber: 0.3g, Sugar: 4.1g, Protein: 39.6g, Sodium: 152mg

POTATO CROQUETTES

Preparation Time: 15 minutes   Cooking Time: 23 minutes   Servings: 4

Ingredients:
- 2 medium Russet potatoes, peeled and cubed
- 2 tablespoons all-purpose flour
- ½ cup Parmesan cheese, grated
- 1 egg yolk
- 2 tablespoons chives, minced
- Pinch of ground nutmeg
- Salt and ground black pepper, as required
- 2 eggs
- ½ cup breadcrumbs
- 2 tablespoons vegetable oil
- Non-stick cooking spray

Directions:
1. In a pan of boiling water, add the potatoes and cook for about 15 minutes.
2. Drain the potatoes well and transfer them into a large bowl.
3. With a potato masher, mash the potatoes and set them aside to cool completely.
4. In the bowl of mashed potatoes, add the flour, Parmesan cheese, egg yolk, chives, nutmeg, salt, and black pepper and mix until well combined.
5. Make small cylinder-shaped croquettes from the mixture.
6. In a shallow dish, crack the eggs and beat well.
7. In another dish, mix the breadcrumbs and oil.
8. Dip the croquettes in egg mixture and then coat with the breadcrumbs mixture.
9. Grease the Air Fryer Basket with cooking spray and arrange in the pot of Instant Pot Duo Crisp.
10. Cover the pot with "Air Fryer Lid" and seal it.
11. Select "Air Fry" and set the temperature to 390 °F for 8 minutes.
12. Press "Start" to begin preheating.
13. When the unit shows "Hot" instead of "On," open the lid and place the croquettes into the basket.
14. Again, cover the pot with "Air Fryer Lid" and seal it.
15. Press "Start" to begin cooking.
16. When cooking time is completed, open the lid transfer the croquettes onto a platter.
17. Serve warm.

Nutritional Information per Serving:
Calories: 283, Fat: 13.4g, Net Carbohydrates: 26.6g, Carbohydrates: 29.9g, Fiber: 3.3g, Sugar: 2.3g, Protein: 11.5g, Sodium: 263mg

CHAPTER 11

DESSERT

WINE POACHED PEARS

Preparation Time: 10 minutes   Cooking Time: 2 hours   Servings: 4

Ingredients:

- 4 ripe pears, peeled
- 1 cup red wine
- ¼ cup sweet vermouth
- ½ cup granulated sugar
- 1 teaspoon salt
- 1 (3-inch) piece orange zest
- 1 vanilla bean, seeds scraped

Directions:

1. Fill the Instant Pot Duo Crisp Air Fryer pot with water up to the ½-full mark.
2. Select "Sous Vide" and set the temperature to 175 °F for 1 hour.
3. Cover the pot with "Pressure Lid" and seal it.
4. Press "Start" to begin preheating.
5. Meanwhile, in a bowl, add all ingredients except for Brussels sprouts and mix until well combined.
6. In a cooking pouch, place all ingredients.
7. Seal the pouch tightly after squeezing out the excess air.
8. When the unit shows "Hot" instead of "On," open the lid and place the pouch in the pot.
9. Again, cover the pot with "Pressure Lid" and seal it.
10. Press "Start" to begin cooking.
11. Open the lid and remove the pouch from the inner pot when the cooking time is completed.
12. Carefully open the pouch and transfer the pears onto serving plates.
13. Drizzle with some of the cooking liquid and serve.

Nutritional Information per Serving:

Calories: 277, Fat: 0.3g, Net Carbohydrates: 52.6g, Carbohydrates: 59.2g, Fiber: 6.6g, Sugar: 4.3g, Protein: 46g, Sodium: 588mg

VANILLA CUSTARD

Preparation Time: 10 minutes   Cooking Time: 2 hours   Servings: 6

Ingredients:

- 1 cup heavy cream
- ½ cup unsweetened almond milk
- ¼ cup sugar
- 2 eggs
- 2 egg yolks
- 1 teaspoon vanilla extract
- ½ teaspoon ground cinnamon
- ¼ teaspoon salt
- Non-stick cooking spray

Directions:

1. In the stand mixer bowl, add all the ingredients and beat on medium-high speed until well combined.
2. Grease 6 (4-ounce) ramekins with cooking spray.
3. Place the mixture into the prepared ramekins evenly, about ¾ of the way full.
4. In the pot of Instant Pot Duo Crisp Air Fryer, arrange the ramekins.
5. Cover the pot with "Air Fryer Lid" and seal it.
6. Select "Slow Cook" and set the time for 2 hours.
7. Press "Start" to begin cooking.
8. When cooking time is completed, open the lid and place the ramekins onto a wire rack to cool for about 1 hour.
9. Refrigerate for about 2 hours before serving.

Nutritional Information per Serving:

Calories: 145, Fat: 10.7g, Net Carbohydrates: 9.4g, Carbohydrates: 9.6g, Fiber: 0.2g, Sugar: 8.6g, Protein: 3.3g, Sodium: 143mg

CHOCOLATE POTS DE CREME

Preparation Time: 10 minutes   **Cooking Time:** 10 minutes   **Servings:** 6

Ingredients:
- 1½ cups heavy cream
- ½ cup milk
- ¼ cup sugar
- 5 large egg yolks
- Pinch of salt
- 8 ounces dark chocolate, melted

Directions:
1. Add the cream and milk to a small pan and bring a gentle simmer.
2. Immediately, remove from the heat.
3. Slowly add the warmed cream mixture into the egg mixture, beating continuously.
4. Divide the mixture into 6 custard cups evenly.
5. With a foil piece, cover each custard cup.
6. In the Instant Pot Duo Crisp Air Fryer pot, place 1 cup of water.
7. Arrange a "Multi-Functional Rack" in the pot.
8. Place 3 custard cups over the rack.
9. Arrange a second rack on top.
10. Place the remaining 3 custard cups on top of the second rack.
11. Cover the pot with "Pressure Lid" and seal it.
12. Select "Pressure" and set the time for 6 minutes.
13. Press "Start" to begin cooking.
14. When cooking time is completed, do a "Natural" release.
15. Open the lid and place the custard cups onto a wire rack.
16. Remove the foil pieces and let them cool.
17. Cover each custard cup with plastic wrap and refrigerate to chill for at least 4 hours before serving.

Nutritional Information per Serving:
Calories: 392, Fat: 26.5g, Net Carbohydrates: 31.8g, Carbohydrates: 33.1g, Fiber: 1.3g, Sugar: 28.8g, Protein: 6.4g, Sodium: 85mg

FRUITY COBBLER

Preparation Time: 15 minutes   **Cooking Time:** 15 minutes   **Servings:** 4

Ingredients:

- 1 plum, pitted and chopped
- 1 apple, cored and chopped
- 1 pear, cored and chopped
- 3 tablespoons coconut oil, melted
- 2 tablespoons raw honey
- ½ teaspoon ground cinnamon
- ¼ cup pecans, chopped
- ¼ cup unsweetened coconut, shredded
- 2 tablespoons sunflower seeds, roasted

Directions:

1. In a bowl, mix all fruit.
2. In the pot of Instant Pot Duo Crisp Air Fryer, place the fruit and drizzle with coconut oil and honey.
3. Sprinkle with cinnamon.
4. Cover the pot with "Pressure Lid" and seal it.
5. Select "Steam" and set the time for 10 minutes.
6. Press "Start" to begin cooking.
7. When cooking time is completed, do a "Quick" release.
8. Open the lid and transfer the cooked fruit into a serving bowl with a slotted spoon.
9. Press "Sauté" of the pot and stir in the pecans, coconut and sunflower seeds.
10. Press "Start" to begin cooking and cook for about 5 minutes, stirring continuously.
11. Press "Cancel" to stop cooking and place the pecan mixture over the cooked fruit.
12. Serve warm.

Nutritional Information per Serving:

Calories: 261, Fat: 18.7g, Net Carbohydrates: 00g, Carbohydrates: 26.1g, Fiber: 4.3g, Sugar: 20.2g, Protein: 1.8g, Sodium: 3mg

CHAPTER 12
SPECIAL EVENTS

CHRISTMAS DINNER CHICKEN

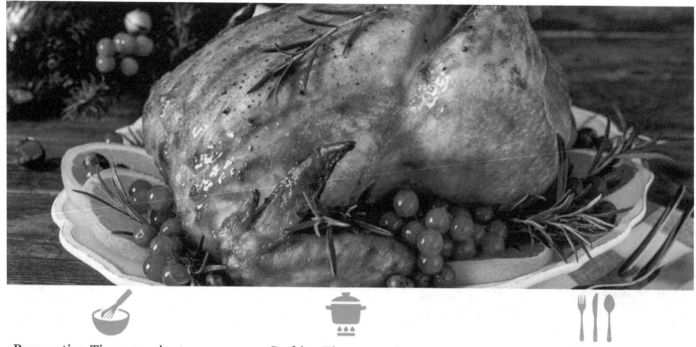

Preparation Time: 15 minutes   Cooking Time: 32 minutes   Servings: 6

Ingredients:

- 1 teaspoon dried basil
- 1 teaspoon dried rosemary
- 1 teaspoon garlic salt
- ½ teaspoon seasoned salt
- 1 (4½-pound) whole chicken, neck and giblets removed
- 1½ cups chicken broth
- Non-stick cooking spray

Directions:

1. Mix the basil, rosemary, garlic salt, and seasoned salt in a bowl.
2. Season the chicken with herb mixture evenly.
3. In the pot of Instant Pot Duo Crisp Air Fryer, pour the chicken broth.
4. Arrange the "Multi-Functional Rack" in the bottom of the pot.
5. Arrange the chicken over the rack.
6. Cover the pot with "Pressure Lid" and seal it.
7. Select "Pressure" and set the time for 22 minutes.
8. Press "Start" to begin cooking.
9. When cooking time is completed, do a "Quick" release.
10. Open the lid and spray the chicken with cooking spray.
11. Now Cover the pot with "Air Fryer Lid" and seal it.
12. Select "Air Fry" and set the temperature to 400 °F for 10 minutes.
13. Press "Start" to begin preheating.
14. When cooking time is completed, open the lid and place the chicken onto a platter for about 10 minutes before carving.
15. Cut the chicken into desired-sized pieces and serve.

Nutritional Information per Serving:

Calories: 658, Fat: 25.6g, Net Carbohydrates: 0.6g, Carbohydrates: 0.7g, Fiber: 0.1g, Sugar: 0.3g, Protein: 99.7g, Sodium: 610mg

EASTER SPECIAL LEG OF LAMB

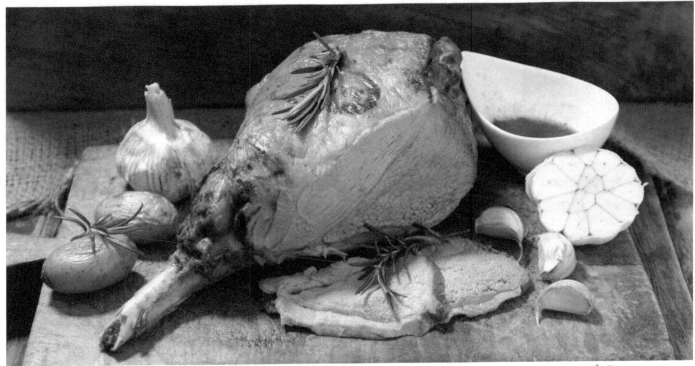

Preparation Time: 15 minutes

Cooking Time: 1¼ hours

Servings: 8

Ingredients:

- 2¼ pounds boneless leg of lamb
- 2 tablespoons olive oil
- Salt and ground black pepper, as required
- 2 fresh rosemary sprigs
- 2 fresh thyme sprigs

Directions:

1. Coat the leg of lamb with oil and sprinkle with salt and black pepper.
2. Wrap the leg of lamb with herb sprigs.
3. Arrange the Multi-Functional Rack in the pot of Instant Pot Duo Crisp.
4. Cover the pot with "Air Fryer Lid" and seal it.
5. Select "Air Fry" and set the temperature to 300 °F for 75 minutes.
6. Press "Start" to begin preheating.
7. When the unit shows "Hot" instead of "On," open the lid and place the leg of lamb over the rack.
8. Again, cover the pot with "Air Fryer Lid" and seal it.
9. Press "Start" to begin cooking.
10. When cooking time is completed, open the lid and place the leg of lamb onto a cutting board.
11. Cut into desired sized pieces and serve.

Nutritional Information per Serving:

Calories: 240, Fat: 13g, Net Carbohydrates: 0.1g, Carbohydrates: 0.5g, Fiber: 0.4g, Sugar: 0g, Protein: 35.9g, Sodium: 117mg

THANKSGIVING MORNING PUMPKIN BREAD

Preparation Time: 15 minutes   Cooking Time: 25 minutes   Servings: 4

Ingredients:

- ¼ cup coconut flour
- 2 tablespoons stevia blend
- 1 teaspoon baking powder
- ¾ teaspoon pumpkin pie spice
- ¼ teaspoon ground cinnamon
- 1/8 teaspoon salt

- ¼ cup canned pumpkin
- 2 large eggs
- 2 tablespoons unsweetened almond milk
- 1 teaspoon vanilla extract
- Non-stick cooking spray

Directions:

1. In a bowl, add the flour, stevia blend, baking powder, spices and salt and mix well
2. Add the pumpkin, eggs, almond milk, and vanilla extract to another large bowl. Beat until well combined.
3. Add the flour mixture and mix until just combined.
4. Line a cake pan with parchment paper and then grease it with cooking spray.
5. Place the mixture into the prepared cake pan evenly.
6. Arrange the "Air Fryer Basket" in the pot of Instant Pot Duo Crisp Air Fryer
7. Cover the pot with "Air Fryer Lid" and seal it.
8. Select "Air Fry" and set the temperature to 350 °F for 25 minutes.
9. Press "Start" to begin preheating.
10. When the unit shows "Hot" instead of "On," open the lid and place the pan into the "Air Fryer Basket."
11. Again, cover the pot with "Air Fryer Lid" and seal it.
12. Press "Start" to begin cooking.
13. When cooking time is completed, open the lid and place the bread pan onto a wire rack for about 5-10 minutes
14. Carefully remove the bread from the pan and place it onto a wire rack to cool completely before slicing.
15. Cut the bread into desired-sized slices and serve.

Nutritional Information per Serving:
Calories: 78, Fat: 3.4g, Net Carbohydrates: 3.9g, Carbohydrates: 7.5g, Fiber: 3.6g, Sugar: 0.9g, Protein: 4.4g, Sodium: 116mg

BIRTHDAY FAVORITE BROWNIE CAKE

Preparation Time: 15 minutes   Cooking Time: 35 minutes   Servings: 6

Ingredients:
- Non-stick cooking spray
- ½ cup dark chocolate chips
- ½ cup butter
- 3 eggs
- ¼ cup sugar
- 1 teaspoon vanilla extract

Directions:
1. Grease a springform pan with cooking spray.
2. In a microwave-safe bowl, add the chocolate chips and butter and microwave for about 1 minute, stirring after every 20 seconds.
3. Remove from the microwave and stir well.
4. Add the eggs, sugar, and vanilla extract to a bowl and blend until light and frothy.
5. Slowly add the chocolate mixture and beat again until well combined.
6. Place the mixture into the prepared springform pan.
7. Arrange a "Multi-Functional Rack" in the pot of the Instant Pot Duo Crisp Air Fryer.
8. Cover the pot with "Air Fryer Lid" and seal it.
9. Select "Air Fry" and set the temperature to 350 °F for 35 minutes.
10. Press "Start" to begin preheating.
11. When the unit shows "Hot" instead of "On," open the lid and place the springform pan over the "Multi-Functional Rack."
12. Again, cover the pot with "Air Fryer Lid" and seal it.
13. Press "Start" to begin cooking.
14. When cooking time is completed, open the lid and place the pan onto a wire rack to cool for about 10 minutes.
15. Carefully invert the cake onto the wire rack to cool completely.
16. Cut the cake into desired-sized slices and serve.

Nutritional Information per Serving:
Calories: 247, Fat: 20.2g, Net Carbohydrates: 15.3g, Carbohydrates: 15.3g, Fiber: 0g, Sugar: 13.9g, Protein: 3.6g, Sodium: 140mg

Conclusion

With that many recipes and a detailed guide to the Instant Pot Duo Crisp Air Fryer, you'll be able to put it to its best use and enjoy a variety of flavorful crispy snacks or delicious dinners in no time. This eleven-in-one multipurpose kitchen wonder has given much-needed peace and comfort to the lives of homemakers, who can now quickly prepare a nutritious and delicious supper for their family. This book's several sections each present a step-by-step approach for preparing a range of meals, including breakfast, chicken, meat, vegetarian, snacks, and much more. So get this latest Instant Pot series hit and start bringing convenience to your kitchen floor right away!

Made in the USA
Coppell, TX
14 March 2022